FREE Test Taking Tips DVD Offer

To help us better serve you, we have developed a Test Taking Tips DVD that we would like to give you for FREE. **This DVD covers world-class test taking tips that you can use to be even more successful when you are taking your test.**

All that we ask is that you email us your feedback about your study guide. Please let us know what you thought about it – whether that is good, bad or indifferent.

To get your **FREE Test Taking Tips DVD**, email freedvd@studyguideteam.com with "FREE DVD" in the subject line and the following information in the body of the email:

   a. The title of your study guide.

   b. Your product rating on a scale of 1-5, with 5 being the highest rating.

   c. Your feedback about the study guide. What did you think of it?

   d. Your full name and shipping address to send your free DVD.

If you have any questions or concerns, please don't hesitate to contact us at freedvd@studyguideteam.com.

Thanks again!

OLSAT Level C Workbook

OLSAT Grade 2 Practice for the
Otis-Lennon School Ability Test
[Gifted and Talented Preparation]

Joshua Rueda

Interested in buying more than 10 copies of our product? Contact us about bulk discounts:
bulkorders@studyguideteam.com

ISBN 13: 9781637752326
ISBN 10: 1637752326

Table of Contents

Quick Overview

As you draw closer to taking your exam, effective preparation becomes more and more important. Thankfully, you have this study guide to help you get ready. Use this guide to help keep your studying on track and refer to it often.

This study guide contains several key sections that will help you be successful on your exam. The guide contains tips for what you should do the night before and the day of the test. Also included are test-taking tips. Knowing the right information is not always enough. Many well-prepared test takers struggle with exams. These tips will help equip you to accurately read, assess, and answer test questions.

A large part of the guide is devoted to showing you what content to expect on the exam and to helping you better understand that content. In this guide are practice test questions so that you can see how well you have grasped the content. Then, answer explanations are provided so that you can understand why you missed certain questions.

Don't try to cram the night before you take your exam. This is not a wise strategy for a few reasons. First, your retention of the information will be low. Your time would be better used by reviewing information you already know rather than trying to learn a lot of new information. Second, you will likely become stressed as you try to gain a large amount of knowledge in a short amount of time. Third, you will be depriving yourself of sleep. So be sure to go to bed at a reasonable time the night before. Being well-rested helps you focus and remain calm.

Be sure to eat a substantial breakfast the morning of the exam. If you are taking the exam in the afternoon, be sure to have a good lunch as well. Being hungry is distracting and can make it difficult to focus. You have hopefully spent lots of time preparing for the exam. Don't let an empty stomach get in the way of success!

When travelling to the testing center, leave earlier than needed. That way, you have a buffer in case you experience any delays. This will help you remain calm and will keep you from missing your appointment time at the testing center.

Be sure to pace yourself during the exam. Don't try to rush through the exam. There is no need to risk performing poorly on the exam just so you can leave the testing center early. Allow yourself to use all of the allotted time if needed.

Remain positive while taking the exam even if you feel like you are performing poorly. Thinking about the content you should have mastered will not help you perform better on the exam.

Once the exam is complete, take some time to relax. Even if you feel that you need to take the exam again, you will be well served by some down time before you begin studying again. It's often easier to convince yourself to study if you know that it will come with a reward!

Test-Taking Strategies

1. Predicting the Answer

When you feel confident in your preparation for a multiple-choice test, try predicting the answer before reading the answer choices. This is especially useful on questions that test objective factual knowledge. By predicting the answer before reading the available choices, you eliminate the possibility that you will be distracted or led astray by an incorrect answer choice. You will feel more confident in your selection if you read the question, predict the answer, and then find your prediction among the answer choices. After using this strategy, be sure to still read all of the answer choices carefully and completely. If you feel unprepared, you should not attempt to predict the answers. This would be a waste of time and an opportunity for your mind to wander in the wrong direction.

2. Reading the Whole Question

Too often, test takers scan a multiple-choice question, recognize a few familiar words, and immediately jump to the answer choices. Test authors are aware of this common impatience, and they will sometimes prey upon it. For instance, a test author might subtly turn the question into a negative, or he or she might redirect the focus of the question right at the end. The only way to avoid falling into these traps is to read the entirety of the question carefully before reading the answer choices.

3. Looking for Wrong Answers

Long and complicated multiple-choice questions can be intimidating. One way to simplify a difficult multiple-choice question is to eliminate all of the answer choices that are clearly wrong. In most sets of answers, there will be at least one selection that can be dismissed right away. If the test is administered on paper, the test taker could draw a line through it to indicate that it may be ignored; otherwise, the test taker will have to perform this operation mentally or on scratch paper. In either case, once the obviously incorrect answers have been eliminated, the remaining choices may be considered. Sometimes identifying the clearly wrong answers will give the test taker some information about the correct answer. For instance, if one of the remaining answer choices is a direct opposite of one of the eliminated answer choices, it may well be the correct answer. The opposite of obviously wrong is obviously right! Of course, this is not always the case. Some answers are obviously incorrect simply because they are irrelevant to the question being asked. Still, identifying and eliminating some incorrect answer choices is a good way to simplify a multiple-choice question.

4. Don't Overanalyze

Anxious test takers often overanalyze questions. When you are nervous, your brain will often run wild, causing you to make associations and discover clues that don't actually exist. If you feel that this may be a problem for you, do whatever you can to slow down during the test. Try taking a deep breath or counting to ten. As you read and consider the question, restrict yourself to the particular words used by the author. Avoid thought tangents about what the author *really* meant, or what he or she was *trying* to say. The only things that matter on a multiple-choice test are the words that are actually in the question. You must avoid reading too much into a multiple-choice question, or supposing that the writer meant something other than what he or she wrote.

5. No Need for Panic

It is wise to learn as many strategies as possible before taking a multiple-choice test, but it is likely that you will come across a few questions for which you simply don't know the answer. In this situation, avoid panicking. Because most multiple-choice tests include dozens of questions, the relative value of a single wrong answer is small. As much as possible, you should compartmentalize each question on a multiple-choice test. In other words, you should not allow your feelings about one question to affect your success on the others. When you find a question that you either don't understand or don't know how to answer, just take a deep breath and do your best. Read the entire question slowly and carefully. Try rephrasing the question a couple of different ways. Then, read all of the answer choices carefully. After eliminating obviously wrong answers, make a selection and move on to the next question.

6. Confusing Answer Choices

When working on a difficult multiple-choice question, there may be a tendency to focus on the answer choices that are the easiest to understand. Many people, whether consciously or not, gravitate to the answer choices that require the least concentration, knowledge, and memory. This is a mistake. When you come across an answer choice that is confusing, you should give it extra attention. A question might be confusing because you do not know the subject matter to which it refers. If this is the case, don't eliminate the answer before you have affirmatively settled on another. When you come across an answer choice of this type, set it aside as you look at the remaining choices. If you can confidently assert that one of the other choices is correct, you can leave the confusing answer aside. Otherwise, you will need to take a moment to try to better understand the confusing answer choice. Rephrasing is one way to tease out the sense of a confusing answer choice.

7. Your First Instinct

Many people struggle with multiple-choice tests because they overthink the questions. If you have studied sufficiently for the test, you should be prepared to trust your first instinct once you have carefully and completely read the question and all of the answer choices. There is a great deal of research suggesting that the mind can come to the correct conclusion very quickly once it has obtained all of the relevant information. At times, it may seem to you as if your intuition is working faster even than your reasoning mind. This may in fact be true. The knowledge you obtain while studying may be retrieved from your subconscious before you have a chance to work out the associations that support it. Verify your instinct by working out the reasons that it should be trusted.

8. Key Words

Many test takers struggle with multiple-choice questions because they have poor reading comprehension skills. Quickly reading and understanding a multiple-choice question requires a mixture of skill and experience. To help with this, try jotting down a few key words and phrases on a piece of scrap paper. Doing this concentrates the process of reading and forces the mind to weigh the relative importance of the question's parts. In selecting words and phrases to write down, the test taker thinks about the question more deeply and carefully. This is especially true for multiple-choice questions that are preceded by a long prompt.

9. Subtle Negatives

One of the oldest tricks in the multiple-choice test writer's book is to subtly reverse the meaning of a question with a word like *not* or *except*. If you are not paying attention to each word in the question, you can easily be led astray by this trick. For instance, a common question format is, "Which of the following is…?" Obviously, if the question instead is, "Which of the following is not…?," then the answer will be quite different. Even worse, the test makers are aware of the potential for this mistake and will include one answer choice that would be correct if the question were not negated or reversed. A test taker who misses the reversal will find what he or she believes to be a correct answer and will be so confident that he or she will fail to reread the question and discover the original error. The only way to avoid this is to practice a wide variety of multiple-choice questions and to pay close attention to each and every word.

10. Reading Every Answer Choice

It may seem obvious, but you should always read every one of the answer choices! Too many test takers fall into the habit of scanning the question and assuming that they understand the question because they recognize a few key words. From there, they pick the first answer choice that answers the question they believe they have read. Test takers who read all of the answer choices might discover that one of the latter answer choices is actually *more* correct. Moreover, reading all of the answer choices can remind you of facts related to the question that can help you arrive at the correct answer. Sometimes, a misstatement or incorrect detail in one of the latter answer choices will trigger your memory of the subject and will enable you to find the right answer. Failing to read all of the answer choices is like not reading all of the items on a restaurant menu: you might miss out on the perfect choice.

11. Spot the Hedges

One of the keys to success on multiple-choice tests is paying close attention to every word. This is never truer than with words like almost, most, some, and sometimes. These words are called "hedges" because they indicate that a statement is not totally true or not true in every place and time. An absolute statement will contain no hedges, but in many subjects, the answers are not always straightforward or absolute. There are always exceptions to the rules in these subjects. For this reason, you should favor those multiple-choice questions that contain hedging language. The presence of qualifying words indicates that the author is taking special care with his or her words, which is certainly important when composing the right answer. After all, there are many ways to be wrong, but there is only one way to be right! For this reason, it is wise to avoid answers that are absolute when taking a multiple-choice test. An absolute answer is one that says things are either all one way or all another. They often include words like *every*, *always*, *best*, and *never*. If you are taking a multiple-choice test in a subject that doesn't lend itself to absolute answers, be on your guard if you see any of these words.

12. Long Answers

In many subject areas, the answers are not simple. As already mentioned, the right answer often requires hedges. Another common feature of the answers to a complex or subjective question are qualifying clauses, which are groups of words that subtly modify the meaning of the sentence. If the question or answer choice describes a rule to which there are exceptions or the subject matter is complicated, ambiguous, or confusing, the correct answer will require many words in order to be expressed clearly and accurately. In essence, you should not be deterred by answer choices that seem excessively long. Oftentimes, the author of the text will not be able to write the correct answer without

offering some qualifications and modifications. Your job is to read the answer choices thoroughly and completely and to select the one that most accurately and precisely answers the question.

13. Restating to Understand

Sometimes, a question on a multiple-choice test is difficult not because of what it asks but because of how it is written. If this is the case, restate the question or answer choice in different words. This process serves a couple of important purposes. First, it forces you to concentrate on the core of the question. In order to rephrase the question accurately, you have to understand it well. Rephrasing the question will concentrate your mind on the key words and ideas. Second, it will present the information to your mind in a fresh way. This process may trigger your memory and render some useful scrap of information picked up while studying.

14. True Statements

Sometimes an answer choice will be true in itself, but it does not answer the question. This is one of the main reasons why it is essential to read the question carefully and completely before proceeding to the answer choices. Too often, test takers skip ahead to the answer choices and look for true statements. Having found one of these, they are content to select it without reference to the question above. Obviously, this provides an easy way for test makers to play tricks. The savvy test taker will always read the entire question before turning to the answer choices. Then, having settled on a correct answer choice, he or she will refer to the original question and ensure that the selected answer is relevant. The mistake of choosing a correct-but-irrelevant answer choice is especially common on questions related to specific pieces of objective knowledge. A prepared test taker will have a wealth of factual knowledge at his or her disposal, and should not be careless in its application.

15. No Patterns

One of the more dangerous ideas that circulates about multiple-choice tests is that the correct answers tend to fall into patterns. These erroneous ideas range from a belief that B and C are the most common right answers, to the idea that an unprepared test-taker should answer "A-B-A-C-A-D-A-B-A." It cannot be emphasized enough that pattern-seeking of this type is exactly the WRONG way to approach a multiple-choice test. To begin with, it is highly unlikely that the test maker will plot the correct answers according to some predetermined pattern. The questions are scrambled and delivered in a random order. Furthermore, even if the test maker was following a pattern in the assignation of correct answers, there is no reason why the test taker would know which pattern he or she was using. Any attempt to discern a pattern in the answer choices is a waste of time and a distraction from the real work of taking the test. A test taker would be much better served by extra preparation before the test than by reliance on a pattern in the answers.

FREE DVD OFFER

Don't forget that doing well on your exam includes both understanding the test content and understanding how to use what you know to do well on the test. We offer a completely FREE Test Taking Tips DVD that covers world class test taking tips that you can use to be even more successful when you are taking your test.

All that we ask is that you email us your feedback about your study guide. To get your **FREE Test Taking Tips DVD**, email freedvd@studyguideteam.com with "FREE DVD" in the subject line and the following information in the body of the email:

- The title of your study guide.
- Your product rating on a scale of 1-5, with 5 being the highest rating.
- Your feedback about the study guide. What did you think of it?
- Your full name and shipping address to send your free DVD.

Verbal Reasoning

Following Directions

In the Following Directions portion of the OLSAT, students will listen to the test administrator give a verbal description of an image and then choose the picture that matches from a group of four similar choices. The challenge is to identify each individual portion of the spoken directions within the image to differentiate between the options and choose the correct answer. This tests students' abilities to listen where an object is in relation to another object as well as words relating to differences in appearance, number, size, and type of object. The Following Directions portion of the OLSAT Level B for first graders consists of twelve multiple-choice questions.

Relevance

Students will practice connecting what they hear to what they see and using descriptive words to differentiate between objects. They will have to follow directions closely to identify minor differences within similar settings.

Tips for Parents

Allow the student ample time to look at each picture as they hear the description so they can begin to eliminate choices that do not match the directions.

Read each instruction several times so that the student can look at each picture individually, measure it against the verbal directions, and move to the next if it does not match.

After the student picks a choice, ask them to identify each descriptive element of the directions within the image to check off all criteria. If their answer was incorrect, this process will help them identify what they missed.

Sample Problem

Choose the picture that shows a cat under a table, a mouse eating cheese, and a wall with stripes.

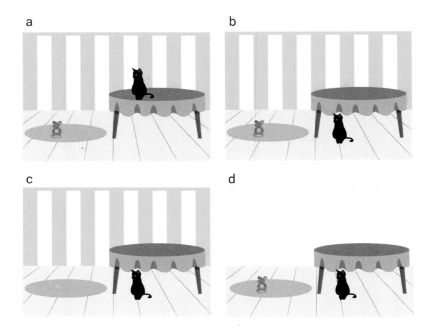

Explanation

The correct answer is Choice *B*. Choice *A* is incorrect because the cat is on top of the table. Choice *C* is incorrect because there is no mouse. Choice *D* is incorrect because there are no stripes on the wallpaper.

Aural Reasoning

In the Aural Reasoning portion of the OLSAT, the test administrator will read a description, and the students will choose the answer that logically solves the question. Each question will have four answer choices listing different objects or steps used to complete common tasks. Images may show just objects and ask students to choose which one should be used given the situation, or they may show the objects in use, in which case the students will choose the image that fits the criteria of the description. This will test the students' abilities to comprehend what is verbally spoken and to recall important details for making logical deductions. Students will be required to know the names and functions of common objects, including tools they may not have come in contact with personally, as questions require the knowledge of general items from different cultures. Students should have an understanding of why a particular response works better than the remaining choices given the verbal description. The students' abilities to logically order events and understand words that denote actions or places will also be tested. The Aural Reasoning portion of the OLSAT consists of twelve multiple-choice questions.

Relevance

Explaining to students how the world around them works will help familiarize them with words used to signify functionality. It also gives them a chance to learn about how things that might not be part of their

everyday lives are used. Children who can listen to a description and identify the steps/tools needed to perform certain tasks tend to be better at grasping concepts and making logical choices. Being able to understand the progression of events make it easier for students to come up with solutions for common problems. When students can mentally picture what is being described to them, they are better able to process events and form reasoned deductions based on what they hear.

Tips for Parents

Have the student explain why the answer they chose makes more sense than the remaining choices.

Explain an additional function or detail about the student's selected choice to further familiarize them with how the object works.

Explain why the incorrect answer choices would not make sense.

Sample Problem

Which item should be used to water flowers in a garden?

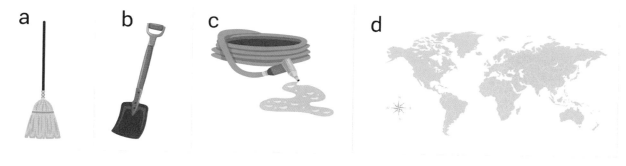

Explanation

The correct answer is Choice *C*. Both Choice *A*, a broom, and Choice *D*, a world map, are not used when gardening. Choice *B*, a shovel, although used when gardening, is not used to water flowers.

Arithmetic Reasoning

In the Arithmetic Reasoning portion of the OLSAT, the test administrator will read a set of directions involving numerical concepts to the students. Students will need to choose one of four choices that correctly solves the question. This tests students' abilities to use descriptions to formulate and solve simple mathematical problems. Questions may require counting, comparing, or performing mathematical operations, such as adding, subtracting, and multiplying. The students' ability to identify what mathematical concept to use for a given problem will also be tested. Although the test may contain simple math problems, the emphasis will be on developing a logical solution to a problem rather than solving basic arithmetic. Students will need to apply mathematical rules, logically sequence, and estimate the outcome of a progression of events. The Arithmetic Reasoning section of the OLSAT test consists of six multiple-choice questions.

Relevance

Grasping mathematical concepts is important to children's understanding of the way problems are sequentially solved. Children should have knowledge of the words used to denote numerical concepts and an ability to interpret and use such language when identifying patterns, solving real-world problems, and making logical predictions. Grasping arithmetic is important in developing the skills used in analyzing and making sense of complex concepts. Children must be able to take the key details from a verbal description and turn them into a logically structured problem. Children should be able to both visualize a description and turn this visualization into a concept that can be generalized and applied to other problems.

Tips for Parents

Allow the student to formulate and write out a numerical equation to better visualize just the arithmetic portion of the verbal description or image.

Before the test, identify key terms that denote mathematical concepts, such as "more than" or "equal to." Encourage the child to listen for these phrases that will help solve the problem.

After the student has selected an answer, repeat the description with an emphasis on all the arithmetic required to complete the problem. This will help the student see the logical progression of the steps.

Sample Problem

In order for the bank workers to open their back safe, two workers need to use three keys each. Which picture shows the total number of keys they will need to open the safe?

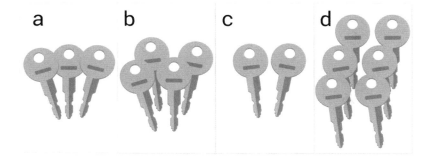

Explanation

The correct answer is Choice *D*. Since each bank worker needs to have three keys, and there are two bank workers, 2 × 3 = 6 keys. Choice *A* is incorrect because it leaves out the detail of there being two workers who each need keys. Choices *B* and *C* also do not show enough keys for each worker to hold three.

Practice Questions

Following Directions

1. Choose the picture that shows a boy on a bike, a truck behind the bike, and a fire hydrant on the sidewalk.

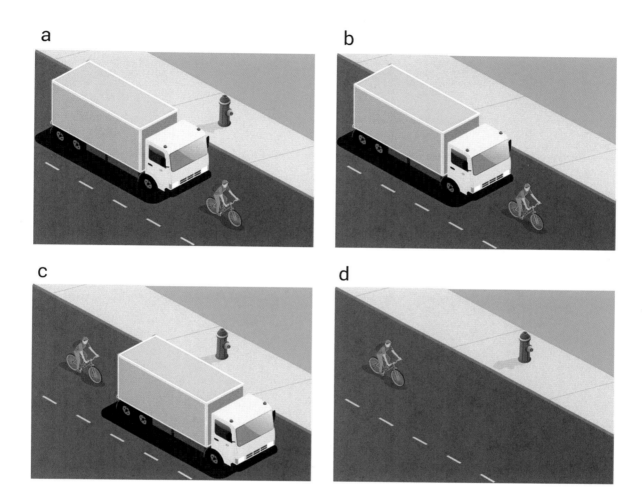

a

b

c

d

2. Which picture shows a lizard with its tongue out, a cactus with a flower on top, and the moon in the background?

a

b

c

d

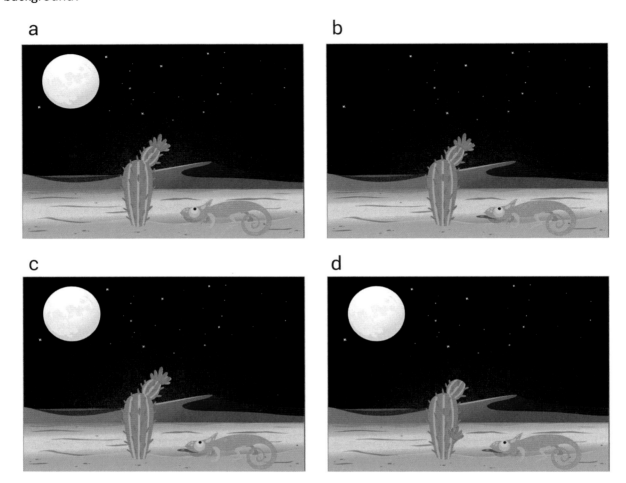

3. Which picture shows a bird in the sky, a large building, and a man wearing a hat?

a

b

c

d

4. In which picture is there a flower with six petals, a bee with a stinger, and a caterpillar crawling on a leaf?

a

b

c

d

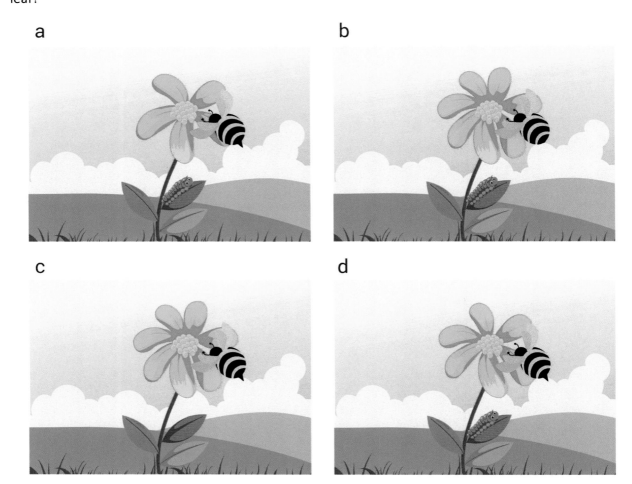

5. Choose the picture that shows a box with a round lid, a bow, and a piece of candy next to the box.

a

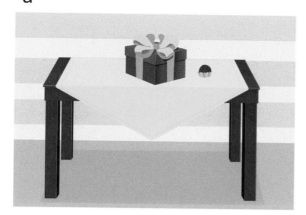

b

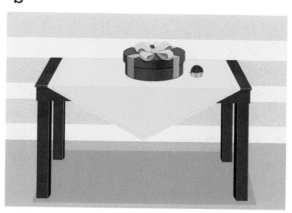

c

d

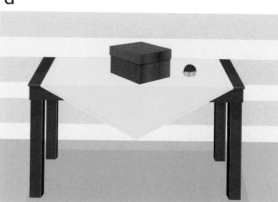

6. In which picture is the yellow car closest to the finish line in first place, the red car in second place, and the blue car in third place?

a

b

c

d

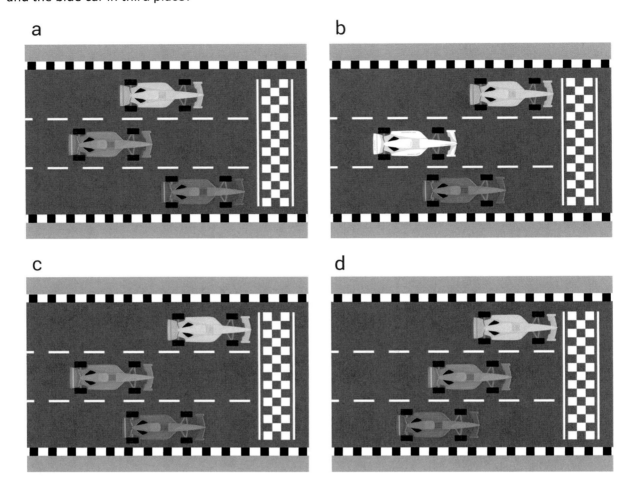

7. Which picture has a frog with neither round nor square spots and a bug flying next to the frog?

a

b

c

d

8. Choose the picture that shows two pillows, a large teddy bear, a poster above the bed, and a pair of shoes in front of the bed.

a

b

c

d

9. Which picture shows a house with two square windows, one round window, a mailbox with its flag up, and a bird on top of the mailbox?

a

b

c

d

10. In which picture is there a painting of a taco to the right of a painting of iced tea and to the left of a painting of nachos?

a

b

c

d

11. Choose the picture where the singer is in the middle of the guitar player and piano player and in front of the drummer.

a

b

c

d

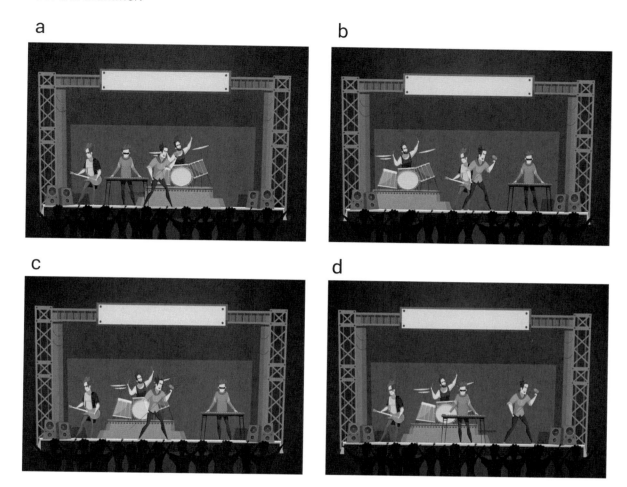

12. In which picture is the second largest dog the third closest to the tennis ball?

a

b

c

d

Aural Reasoning

1. Which item would be used to remove the wrinkles from a shirt?

a   b   c   d

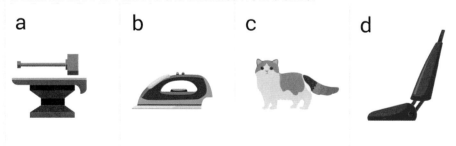

2. Which animal likes to spend its time running on a wheel?

a   b   c   d

3. Which bug makes honey?

a b   c   d

4. Which item is used in the rain to keep people from getting wet?

a b c   d

5. Which article of clothing should be worn in the snow?

a b c d

6. Which item do baseball players use to catch the ball?

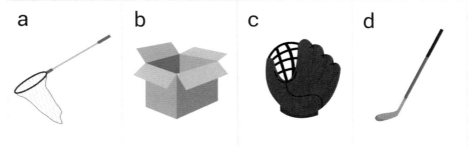

7. Which item do tennis players use to hit tennis balls over the net?

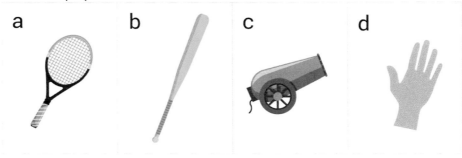

8. Which picture shows a person talking on the phone while driving a car?

a

b

c

d

9. Which picture shows a person who is neither skiing nor surfing?

a

b

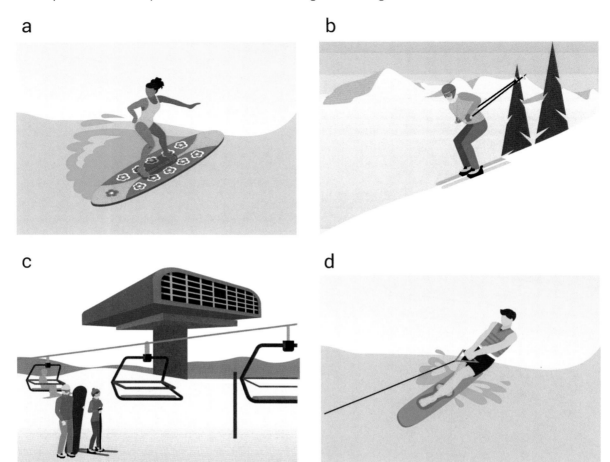

c

d

10. Which picture shows a person who is running but not sweating?

a

b

c

d

11. When Lisa gets home from school, she always has the same routine. First, she takes off her shoes, then she empties her pockets, and then she does her homework before finally watching TV. What is the second thing Lisa does when she gets home from school?

a

b

c

d

12. Avery never eats dinner before he walks his dog. He also never walks his dog before he takes a shower. Which of the following does Avery do last?

a

b

c

d

Arithmetic Reasoning

1. There is a picture of five cats. Which picture contains two fewer cats?

a   b   c   d

2. There is a picture of eight pieces of candy. Which picture shows one more piece of candy?

a   b   c   d

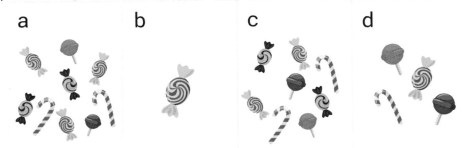

3. There is a picture of three library books. Which picture contains one more library book?

a   b   c   d

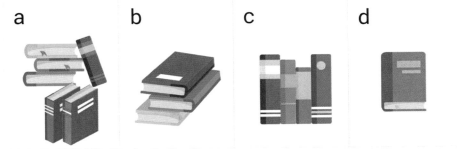

4. There is a picture of ten coins. In which image are there two fewer coins?

a   b   c   d

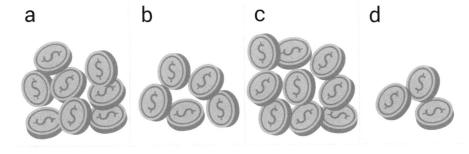

5. There is a picture of two cars. Which image shows one more car?

a   b   c   d

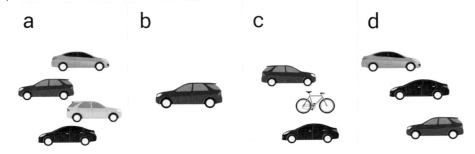

6. There is a picture of four pairs of shoes (eight shoes total). In which picture are there two fewer pairs of shoes?

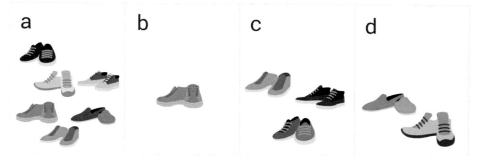

Answer Explanations

Following Directions

1. A: Choice A matches all the criteria in the directions: There is a boy on a bike, a truck behind the bike, and a fire hydrant on the sidewalk. When comparing the directions with the other images, Choice *B* has no fire hydrant, and Choice *D* has no truck. Choice *C* has all the objects needed, but the truck is in front of the boy on a bike.

2. C: The first picture, Choice *A*, has all the objects described in the directions, but the lizard is not sticking out its tongue. Choice *B* does not have a moon. Choice *D* is incorrect because the flower is in the wrong place.

3. C: Both Choices *A* and *D* are incorrect because they do not have the bird described. Additionally, the building in Choice *A* is not as large as it is in the other drawings. Choice *B* is incorrect because the man is not wearing a hat.

4. D: Choices *A*, *B*, and *C* are incorrect because the flowers shown do not have the correct number of petals. Additionally, the bee in Choice *B* has no stinger, and Choice *C* does not have a caterpillar.

5. B: Both Choices *A* and *D* are incorrect because the box does not have a round lid. Choice *C* does not have the candy described.

6. C: In Choice *A*, the yellow car is not closest to the finish line, so it is incorrect. There is no blue car in Choice *B*, so it is incorrect. The red car is in third place in Choice *D*, so it is incorrect. Only in Choice *C* is the yellow car in first place, the red car in second, and the blue car in last.

7. A: Choices *B* and *D* both contain frogs with spots, so they are incorrect. Although Choices *A* and *C* both have frogs with no spots, Choice *C* does not have the bug described.

8. B: Choice *A* is incorrect because it has three pillows and the bear is smaller than in the other choices. In Choice *B*, the student can identify all elements from the directions. When compared with the remaining choices, Choice *C* has a different placement for the shoes, and Choice *D* lacks the poster.

9. D: Choice *A* has two round windows instead of one. The mailbox in Choice *B* does not have its flag up, and the bird in Choice *C* is not on top of the right object. Even though all choices have the correct objects, only Choice *D* has all the required objects in the right places.

10. D: Locating the taco painting's position in each picture will help the student eliminate the incorrect choices. Choice *A* is incorrect because the taco is to the left of the iced tea, and Choice *C* is incorrect because there is no taco painting. While Choices *B* and *D* both display the taco to the right of the iced tea, only Choice *D* shows the taco to the left of the nachos.

11. C: In Choices *A* and *D*, the singer is not between the guitar and piano players. In Choice *B*, he is between them but not in front of the drummer. Therefore, Choice *C* is the only image that displays the singer in front of the drummer and between the guitar and piano players.

12. C: Because Choice *A* shows a bone instead of a tennis ball, it is incorrect. The middle-sized dog must be farthest away from the tennis ball to be in the "third closest" position. Choice *B* shows the smallest dog in the last position, and Choice *D* shows the biggest dog, leaving only Choice *C*.

Aural Reasoning

1. B: Only the iron can remove wrinkles from a shirt. Choices *A*, *C*, and *D* are objects unrelated to the chore.

2. B: Choice *A* is incorrect because a bird spends most of its time flying. Choice *D* is not the type of animal to run on a wheel for long periods of time. Although Choices *B* and *C*, a hamster and a dog, both love to run, the hamster is the only animal commonly known to run on a wheel.

3. D: Only the bee is capable of producing honey out of nectar it collects from flowers. Choice *A*, a butterfly, also pollinates flowers, but it does not produce honey. Choices *B* and *C*, a spider and a beetle, do not produce honey. Therefore, Choice *D* is correct.

4. D: Umbrellas have a specific shape designed to protect the holder from rain. Choice *A*, a walking cane, would be too thin, and Choice *C*, tennis shoes, only cover the feet. Choice *B*, swim trunks, are for swimming, not for going out in the rain; therefore, only Choice *D*, an umbrella, works to keep people from getting wet in the rain.

5. A: The only option that would keep one warm in the snow would be Choice *A*, the snow jacket. Choices *B*, *C*, and *D*—a tank top, jeans, and sandals— are more suitable for a warmer day because they do not provide enough protection from the cold.

6. C: Baseball players use a mitt to protect their hands when catching high-speed baseballs. Choices *A* and *B*, a fishing net and cardboard box, are not used on a baseball field. Choice *D*, a hockey stick, is used in hockey, not baseball.

7. A: Tennis players use rackets designed to hit tennis balls with careful aim. Although Choices *B*, *C*, and *D*—a baseball bat, cannon, and hand—could send a tennis ball across the net, they are not designed specifically for this purpose.

8. D: Choice *B* is incorrect because there is no car, and Choice *C* is incorrect because there is no phone. Choices *A* and *D* both have someone driving and someone talking on the phone, but only in Choice *D* is the same person doing both.

9. C: Choices *A*, *B*, and *D* are incorrect because the images show people who are actively skiing or surfing. The person in Choice *C* is waiting to ski but is not skiing yet. Therefore, Choice *C* is correct.

10. C: Choices *B* and *D* are incorrect because the person pictured is not running. Choice *A* is incorrect because the person is sweating; therefore, Choice *C* is correct.

11. D: The second item on the list of things Lisa does after she gets home from school is empty her pockets. Choice *A* shows Lisa taking off her shoes, which is the first thing she does. Choice *B* shows her doing homework, which is her third task. Choice *C* shows her playing video games, which is not on the list at all. Choice *D* shows her emptying her pockets, which is the remaining and correct answer.

12. B: Avery takes a shower (Choice *A*) before he walks his dog (Choice *D*), which comes before he eats dinner (Choice *B*). Therefore, eating dinner is the last thing he does, so Choice *B* is the correct answer.

Arithmetic Reasoning

1. B: Starting with five cats and subtracting two, leaves three cats (5 – 2 = 3). Therefore, Choice *B* is correct because it contains three cats.

2. A: Starting with eight pieces of candy and adding one gives a total of nine pieces (8 + 1 = 9). This leaves Choice *A* as the image with the correct number of candy pieces.

3. C: The original image contains three books, and adding one more gives a total of four books (3 + 1 = 4). Only Choice *C* contains the correct amount of four books.

4. A: Starting with ten coins and subtracting two leaves eight coins (10 – 2 = 8). This means Choice *A* is the correct answer.

5. D: Adding one car to the original image of two gives a total of three cars (2 + 1 = 3). This eliminates Choices *A* and *B*. Although Choice *C* has three objects, it is incorrect because there are still only two cars. Only Choice *D* has exactly three cars.

6. D: This question specifically refers to pairs of shoes, not individual shoes. If the original image contains four pairs of shoes and two pairs are subtracted, that leaves two pairs of shoes (4 – 2 = 2). Choice *A* added two pairs of shoes, and Choice *B* subtracted three. Choice *C* contains two fewer individual shoes but only one less pair. Choice *D* has only two pairs of shoes, so it is the correct answer.

Nonverbal Reasoning

Picture Classification

In the Picture Classification portion of the OLSAT, students will analyze four different images. They will compare and contrast the pictures to determine which image is not like the others. There will be no spoken instructions; students will only be provided with the pictures and the prompt. This section will test students' abilities to recognize patterns and classify images. Differences in color, size, number, theme, and pattern will be presented. The students' ability to identify the use and name of the object pictured will also be tested. The students will need to be familiar with the way objects are organized and categorized in the world. The Picture Classification portion of the OLSAT test is one of three categories of Pictorial Reasoning questions, which measure students' ability to reason with images rather than verbal descriptions. Therefore, students will need a basic understanding of how to recognize patterns and classify objects based on sight alone.

Relevance

The ability to recognize visual differences can help children organize and interpret the visual stimuli and sensory data they experience on a daily basis. If they can sort ideas and images by similarity and recognize when one does not fit into a particular group, then they will have an easier time understanding images they have never encountered. Recognition of patterns also allows children to visualize and logically process sequences.

Tips for Parents

Have the child identify what is similar in each image in order to spot the one that does not contain the similarity.

Allow the student to describe each image verbally in order to get the entire picture and ensure no key details are left out.

Tell the student to look carefully at each image before determining the answer. This allows them to take in all the images and classify them as a group before determining which one does not belong.

Sample Problem

Which picture does not belong with the others?

a b c d

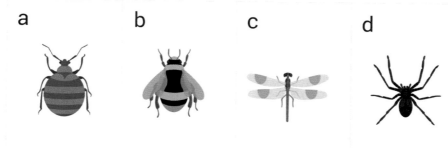

Explanation

The correct answer is Choice *D*. Each image contains a bug of some sort. Counting the bugs' legs reveals that Choices *A*, *B*, and *C* all have six legs. The spider is an arachnid, the only non-insect, meaning it has eight legs instead of six.

Picture Analogies

In the Picture Analogies portion of the OLSAT, students need to match a given image with another image that is the most similar from four options. This section tests the ability to identify similarities rather than differences between images. Questions will consist of comparisons between both visual patterns and categories of objects. Students should be able to classify objects and determine similarities in positioning and perspective. Students must visually identify similarities without the use of detailed verbal instructions. They will use only the images given when determining their answer. This will test the students' understanding of the way images are compared and contrasted to group together similar items. The Picture Analogies portion of the test is the second Pictorial Reasoning section in which students use visual cues to identify patterns.

Relevance

Children who can identify similarities in seemingly different images are better able to organize their thoughts in a way that helps them remember what they have seen. Classifying information helps children better understand the functions of items and how they interact with each other. As children strengthen the ability to identify similarities, they will gain confidence in understanding new visual stimuli through comparison to images seen in the past. The better children understand connections between visual stimuli, the more they will be able to understand and define the world around them.

Tips for Parents

Have the student identify the theme of each image set to help them identify possible similarities.

Give the student enough time to examine all possible choices. Have them explain why the incorrect answers do not match.

Tell the student to name each object pictured so they can practice naming objects in relation to each other.

Sample Problem

There are four boxes. In the top left corner is an image of a book that is open. In the top right is an image of a closed book. In the bottom left corner is the image of a brown cardboard box that is open.

The bottom right corner is blank. The pictures in the top boxes are similar. Choose the image that is comparable to the bottom picture in the same way the pictures at the top are related.

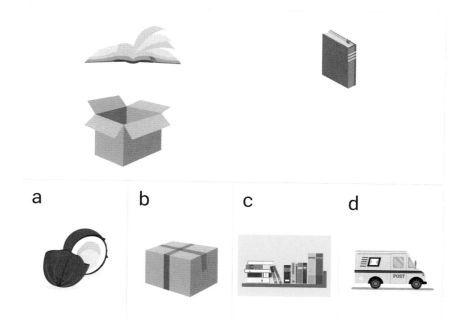

Explanation

The correct answer is Choice *B* because it shows a closed box just as the book above it is closed. First, identify the difference between the top two images; the book is open in one picture and closed in the next. Then notice the similarity between the bottom image of the box and the image of the book above it; they are both open. Therefore, the remaining panel needs a box that matches the image of the closed book above it.

Figural Classification

In the Figural Classification portion of the OLSAT, students will see four images. They will compare and contrast the images and determine which one does not match the theme of the others. Pictures will show figures and abstract shapes, not necessarily real objects. Students will need to identify differences in the figures, such as size, pattern, shape, position, color, and number. There will be a common pattern between the figures, and only one figure will not match the others in a specific way. There will be no verbal instructions given to the students; they will need to determine the correct answer through the images only. The student will need a basic understanding of pattern recognition in order to identify changes in form. Figural Classification is a section of Figural Reasoning questioning, which differs from pictorial classification because it presents abstract images without proper names. Students will no longer be able to identify differences based on function; they must rely on visual representation only.

Relevance

Noticing differences in patterns helps children recognize and process new visual data. It also helps them organize their thoughts into more easily understood patterns. Being able to identify differences in abstract images allows the students' imaginations to expand beyond common objects. This helps them identify patterns based on the purely visual elements of an image. When children can notice patterns outside of any exterior functionality, their imaginations can form more unique pattern combinations, and they can better work with images outside the confines of space and time.

Tips for Parents

Have the student start with a simple comparison like the shapes of the figures presented. Then have them compare each image with a different theme like color or size until they have narrowed down the one image that does not belong.

Have the student draw their own unique that would fit with the theme of the images given in order to further understand the pattern.

Have the student point out which part of the chosen image does not match the remaining answers and identify what would have to change for it to fit with the others.

Sample Problem

Which figure does not belong with the others?

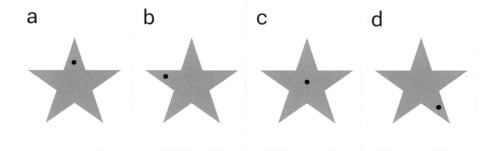

Explanation

The correct answer is Choice *C*. Each image depicts a star containing a small dot inside of it at different positions. However, in Choice *C* the black dot is not at one of the star's tips.

Figural Analogies

The Figural Analogies section prompts students to recognize relationships using geometric shapes. Each question presents four squares, three of which contain shapes/shading and one of which is empty. Students should identify the relationship among the squares and determine which answer choice belongs in the empty one. One technique would be to visualize each answer choice in the empty square and decide if the relationship is consistent with the rest of the squares. This section requires students to comprehend both shapes and shading to visualize analogous relationships. The relationship in one row (or column) will have an analogous, or comparable, relationship in the next row (or column).

Relevance

How are Figural Analogies related to intelligence? **Analogy** compares two objects, and the viewer must recognize the relationship between those objects. Analogical reasoning not only helps individuals understand relationships between things, but it also asks them to remember relationships that they can for future comparisons. Analogical reasoning is necessary to human thought, and some even consider it

a basis for human thought. Think of it like this: a teacher is trying to explain the concept of a "family tree." The students do not understand what the teacher is talking about, so she decides to use an analogy to explain. She gets out a single bunch of grapes and says, "These two grapes at the top are a mom and dad. The five grapes coming from the mom and dad grapes are their children. The grapes along this stem horizontal from the mom and dad are the mom's siblings," and so on. The concept clicks in the students' minds because the teacher used an analogy. She showed a similar relationship within another familiar space, and since the students understood this primary relationship, they could apply it to the new relationship. Analogies can help people learn and understand concepts within the world.

Tips for Parents

Start by guiding your student through some questions before they do the problems independently. Direct them to the top row and help them identify the relationship between the two squares. Ask them to look at the bottom row and choose the answer that will complete the row using the same pattern as the top. Have the student explain why the square they chose completed the relationship. Do this for several problems before letting the student proceed on their own. They will silently start to ask themselves about the relationships between the rows.

Sample Problem

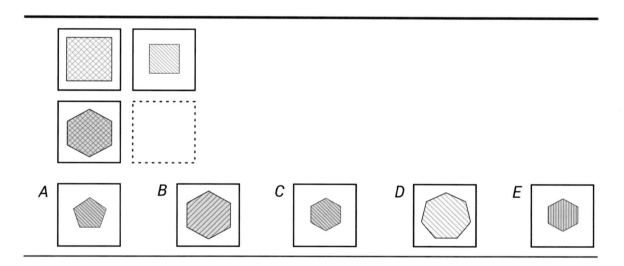

Explanation

The correct answer is Choice *C*. Looking at the first row, one can see that the images are related in shape, size, and pattern. They are both squares, but the one on the left is bigger. The pattern in the first square is checkered, while the pattern in the second square is diagonal lines. In the bottom pair, the correct answer should be the same shape but smaller. That leaves Choices *C* and *E* as possibilities. The correct answer should also have a diagonal line pattern, making Choice *E* incorrect because its lines are vertical.

Pattern Matrix

In the Pattern Matrix section, students will see a three-by-three grid with one empty box. The contents of each box will vary based on shape, color, and/or rotation. Each row and column contains a serial pattern, and the student must figure out which shape belongs in the empty box to complete the pattern.

Studying Figural Analogy questions will help students prepare for Pattern Matrix questions because the two sections are similar in presentation. Students will have to use the same skills of comparison and pattern recognition for both sections. The difference is that Pattern Matrix utilizes a more complex grid sequence. Essentially, Pattern Matrix tests students' abilities to find the missing element within a matrix of geometric shapes.

Relevance

How is Pattern Matrix related to intelligence? While this exam utilizes patterns in shape and size, pattern matrices also exist within language and reasoning. Serial reasoning within language begins with one statement, which supports a second statement, which supports a third statement. For example:

> I'm staying inside because it's so cold outside, so you have to stay inside too.
>
> Statement 1: It's so cold outside.
>
> (Supports) Statement 2: I'm staying inside.
>
> (Supports) Statement 3: You have to stay inside too.

Similarly, Pattern Matrix requires students to utilize patterns of reasoning. They must look at the patterns existing in the matrix as a whole to determine which answer choice goes in the blank space. Just as a pattern of statements leads to a conclusion, so do the visual patterns within the matrix. Students can determine the missing square by looking at the surrounding boxes and identifying how it fits within the whole image.

Tips for Parents

Guide your child through a problem by asking questions. Have them look at each row and ask them to identify how the image changes in each box, then do the same for each column. Encourage them to note the changes out loud because a word pattern may help lead them to the correct answer. Do four or five of these with your student, asking them the same question. Then, let them do the rest alone. They should be asking themselves the same question, moving across and down the image to find the pattern, and ultimately finding the missing square.

Sample Problem

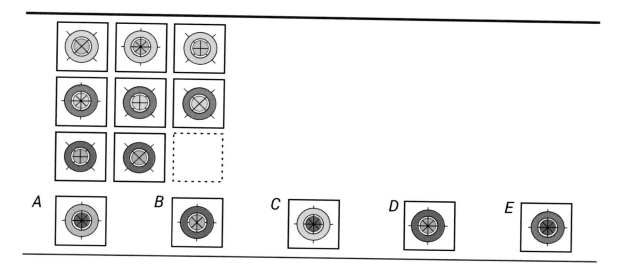

Explanation

The matrix above contains a pattern in each row and column based on the divisions within each image's inner circle. The first two rows and columns contain one circle divided into four pieces forming an "x," one circle divided into four pieces forming a "+," and one circle divided into eight pieces. The final row/column is missing an inner circle divided into eight pieces, so the correct answer choice is *D*.

Figural Series

In the Figural Series portion of the OLSAT, students will need to finish a sequence of shapes. They will see a series of four shapes with a common theme and choose the figure that logically completes the series from a list of four choices. These figures will be abstract shapes that do not particularly correspond to a real-world item. This will test students' ability to identify similarities and differences between the figures based on appearance alone. Students should be able to recognize pattern variation in size, shape, number, shading, and position of figures. The Figural Series questions rely on visuals alone; there will be little to no verbal instruction.

Relevance

Recognizing and completing patterns with only visual cues sharpens children's reasoning and ability to find logical progressions. If children can identify patterns and common themes among abstract shapes, then they will have an easier time ordering and classifying other images. A strengthened ability to form deductions based on logical progressions will help children better process and convey ideas in an organized, understandable way.

Tips for Parents

Have the student identify similarities between the first two images, then between those images and the third image, and so on. This may help them spot the pattern earlier and enable them to focus on its progression.

Have the student draw their own figure of how the pattern would progress after the correct answer.

Encourage the student to focus on one element of the pattern at a time, such as shape, and then move on to another element until they recognize each aspect of the pattern.

Sample Problem

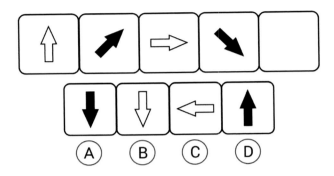

Explanation

The correct answer is Choice *B*. In each panel, the arrow changes position to move slightly clockwise. Therefore, the correct answer will show an arrow that has shifted the slightly clockwise from the last panel. Additionally, the color of the arrow alternates between black and white. Since the last panel contains a black arrow, the correct answer needs to be a white arrow.

Practice Questions

Picture Classification

1.

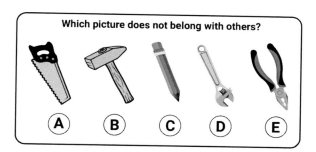

2.

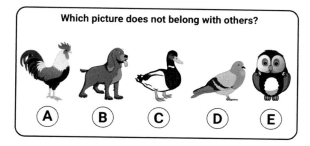

3.

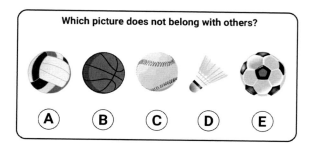

4.

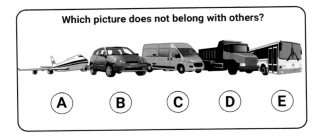

Which picture does not belong with others?

A B C D E

5.

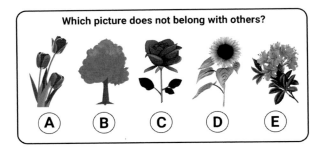

Which picture does not belong with others?

A B C D E

Picture Analogies

For the questions below, choose the picture that comes next.

1.

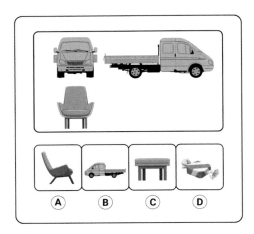

A B C D

2.

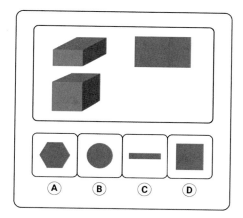

3.

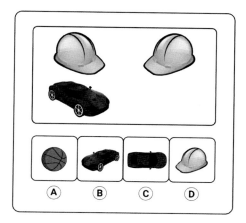

4.

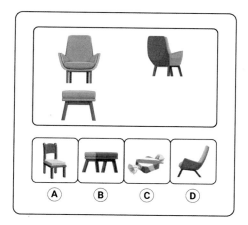

Figural Classification

1.

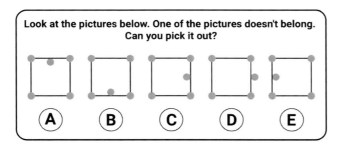

2.

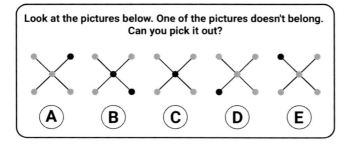

3.

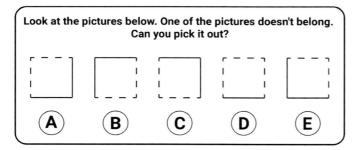

4.

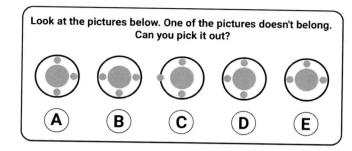

5.

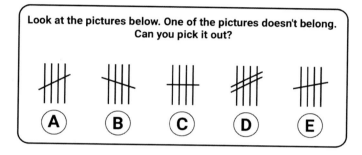

6.

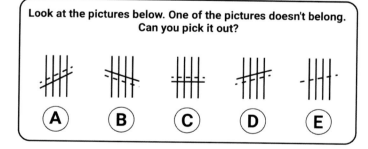

7.

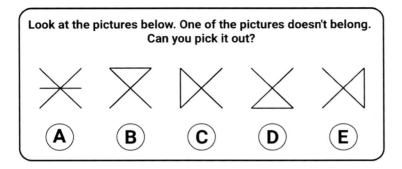

Look at the pictures below. One of the pictures doesn't belong.
Can you pick it out?

A   B   C   D   E

Figural Analogies

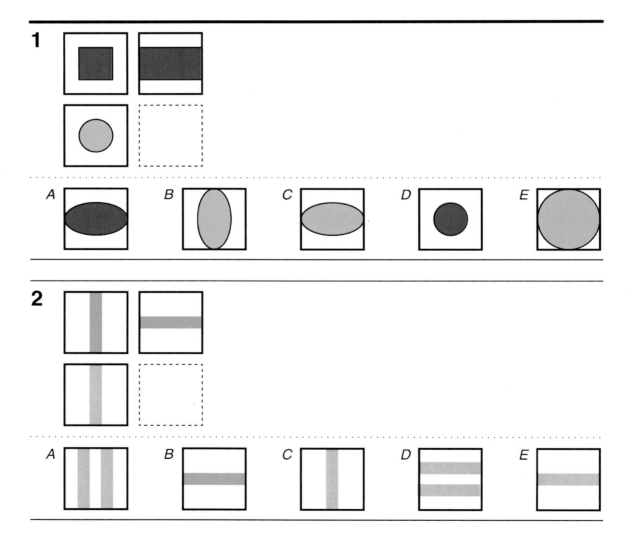

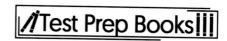

3

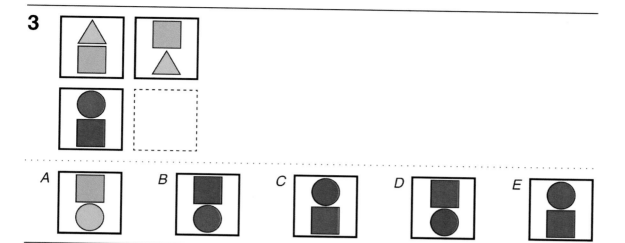

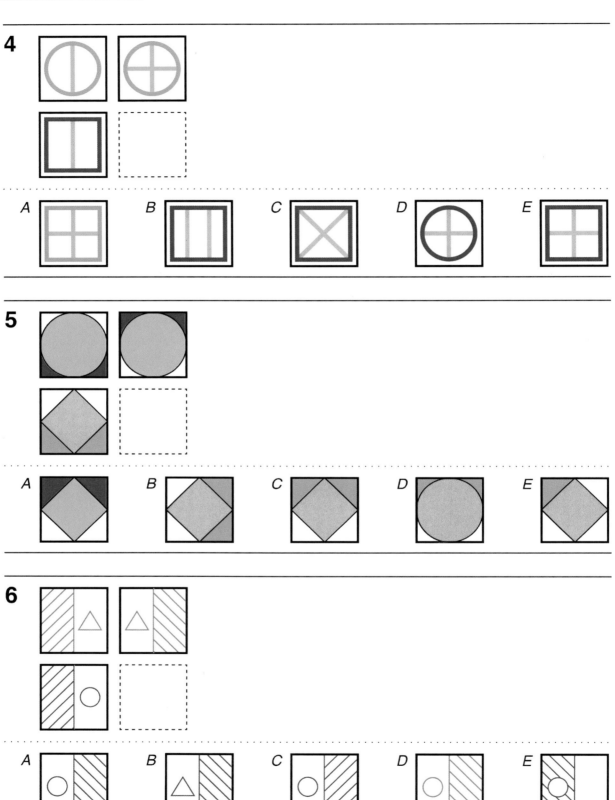

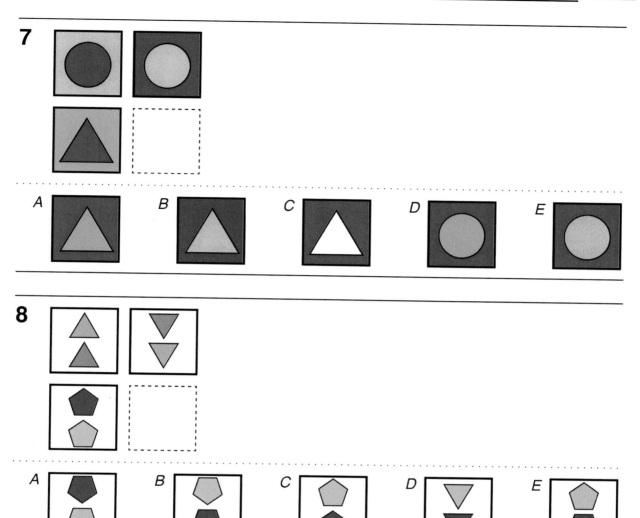

Pattern Matrix

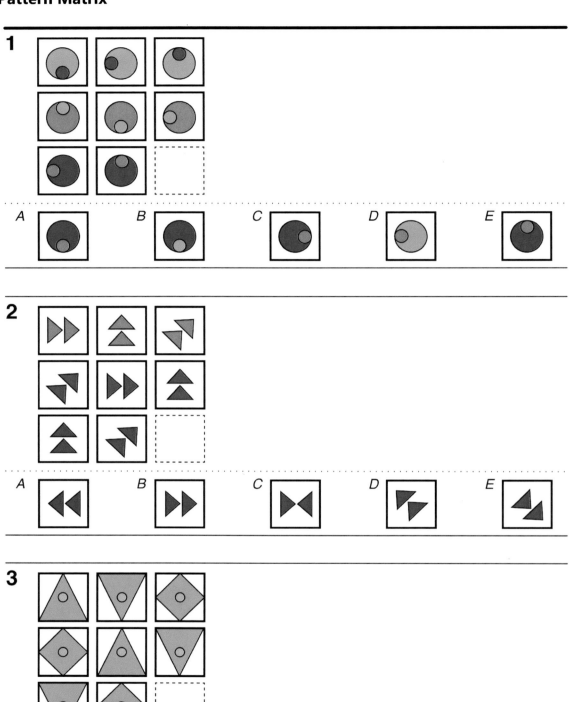

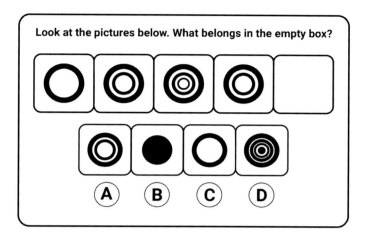

Figural Series

1.

2.

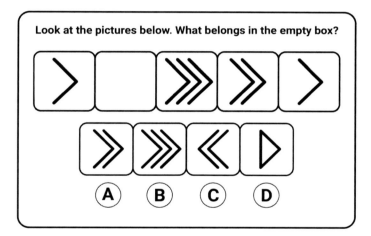

3.

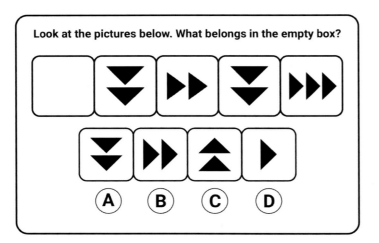

Answer Explanations

Picture Classification

1. C: The choices are a saw, hammer, pencil, wrench, and pliers. All choices are construction tools except for Choice C, the pencil.

2. B: The pictures show a chicken, dog, duck, pigeon, and owl. Choices A, C, D, and E feature pictures of birds, while Choice B features a dog.

3. D: The pictures show a volleyball, basketball, baseball, badminton birdie, and soccer ball. All answer choices are balls except for Choice D.

4. A: The pictures show an airplane, car, van, truck, and bus. All the pictures are of ground transportation except for Choice A, the airplane.

5. B: Choices A, C, D, and E are images of flowers. The only image that does not belong is Choice B, a tree.

Picture Analogies

1. A: The top two images show a front-facing truck followed by a right-facing truck. The second row shows a front-facing chair. To match the pattern from the top, the correct answer needs to be a right-facing chair, or Choice A.

2. D: The top two images show a rectangle in 3D, then a rectangle in 2D. The bottom image shows a square in 3D. Only Choice D, a square in 2D, can complete the analogy.

3. B: The top row shows a hat turned toward the right, then the same hat turned toward the left. The bottom row shows a car turned toward the right. The correct answer must be a car turned toward the left, or Choice B.

4. B: The top row shows two chairs, one facing forward and the other angled backwards. The bottom row shows an ottoman. Choice B shows an ottoman angled backwards, so this is the correct answer.

Figural Classification

1. D: Each figure has five dots. Each figure has five dots. In Choices A, B, C, and E, there is one dot on each corner and one dot on the inside of the square. Choice D features one dot on the outside of the square, making it different than the others.

2. B: Each figure has five dots. In Choice B, two dots are black, and three dots are gray. This makes Choice B different than the other figures, which have one black dot and four gray dots.

3. D: All figures make up a square. Choices A, B, C, and E feature two solid lines and two dashed lines. Choice D features one solid line and three dashed lines, making it different from the others.

4. C: Choice C does not belong with the others because one of its solid gray circles overlaps the outer circle. The solid gray circles in the other figures are inside the outer circle.

5. D: Choice *D* features two lines going through four vertical lines. The other answer choices show one line going through four vertical lines. Thus, Choice *D* is different from the others.

6. E: Choices *A*, *B*, *C*, and *D* have both a solid and a dashed line going through four vertical lines. Choice *E* shows one dashed line going through four vertical lines. Since Choice *E* is missing the solid line, it is different from the others.

7. A: Choice *A* does not belong because, unlike the rest of the images, it does not contain a closed triangle.

Figural Analogies

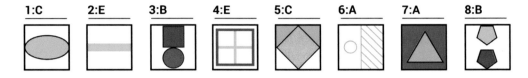

Pattern Matrix

Figural Series

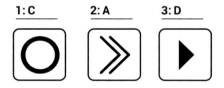

Dear OLSAT Level C customer,

We would like to start by thanking you for purchasing this study guide for the OLSAT Level C exam. We hope that we exceeded your expectations.

Our goal in creating this study guide was to cover all of the topics that you will see on the test. We also strove to make our practice questions as similar as possible to what you will encounter on test day. With that being said, if you found something that you feel was not up to your standards, please send us an email and let us know.

We would also like to let you know about other books in our catalog that may interest you.

Common Core Math Grade 2

This can be found on Amazon: amazon.com/dp/1628456450

NNAT Grade 2 Level C

amazon.com/dp/1628458925

We have study guides in a wide variety of fields. If the one you are looking for isn't listed above, then try searching for it on Amazon or send us an email.

Thanks Again and Happy Testing!
Product Development Team
info@studyguideteam.com

FREE Test Taking Tips DVD Offer

To help us better serve you, we have developed a Test Taking Tips DVD that we would like to give you for FREE. **This DVD covers world-class test taking tips that you can use to be even more successful when you are taking your test.**

All that we ask is that you email us your feedback about your study guide. Please let us know what you thought about it – whether that is good, bad or indifferent.

To get your **FREE Test Taking Tips DVD**, email freedvd@studyguideteam.com with "FREE DVD" in the subject line and the following information in the body of the email:

a. The title of your study guide.

b. Your product rating on a scale of 1-5, with 5 being the highest rating.

c. Your feedback about the study guide. What did you think of it?

d. Your full name and shipping address to send your free DVD.

If you have any questions or concerns, please don't hesitate to contact us at freedvd@studyguideteam.com.

Thanks again!

Made in the USA
Las Vegas, NV
24 February 2025

18669907R00040